VOICE STRATEGY

CREATING USEFUL AND USABLE VOICE EXPERIENCES

VOICE STRATEGY

CREATING USEFUL AND USABLE VOICE EXPERIENCES

By

SUSAN & SCOT WESTWATER

First Edition: November 2019
Printed in the United States of America
ISBN: 978-1675235034

WE WOULD LIKE TO THANK

Pete Erickson, Bradley Metrock, James Poulter, Jen Heape, Heidi Culbertson, Ahmed Bouzid, Brielle Nickoloff and the entire Voice community for welcoming us with open arms and allowing us to teach, learn and grow.

To all of our family and friends (especially the grandmas), we wouldn't be here if it wasn't for your love, support and at times, babysitting - we are eternally grateful.

SUSAN WOULD LIKE TO THANK

My husband Scot for his constant support and for reminding me the only way to expand my comfort zone is to do something outside of it.

Carrie Hane for her sage advice and helping me to realize that sometimes, it is okay to get out of my lane.

Rebecca Evanhoe for her encouragement to write this book and for inspiring the Voice First Unicorn.

SCOT WOULD LIKE TO THANK

My wife Susan for joining me on this adventure and helping me find my true calling

Gary Vaynerchuck for "giving us the permission to go all in on ourselves" and bringing the opportunity of Voice to our attention in 2017.

Fraser Cameron for showing me there's more to life than a traditional 9-5 and helping me become an epic dad.

A SPECIAL THANK YOU TO OUR EARLY SUPPORTERS

Alichia Sawitoski	Jeremy Bokor
Audrey Batigne	Karen Groene
Benn Cheney	Kelly Williams
Bradley Metrock	Lee Parkel
Brett Adler	Michal Stanislawek
Caleb Gates	Paivi Tuomi
Chris Bonney	Sella Yoffe
Curt Mercadante	Sirish Kondabolu
Dyung Ngo	Stuart Crane
Elijah Jackson	Terrence Brown
Janaina da Silva Pereira	Wally Mostafa

TABLE OF CONTENTS

Section 3: The Importance Of Being

Useful & Usable

Section 4: How To Get Started With Creating

Valuable Experiences

Section 5: Shaping Your Strategy With The Voice Experience Framework

Considerations For Creating Voice Experiences

References

INTRODUCTION

We talk a lot in this book about being customer centric because it's critical for success in today's consumer attention landscape. There's a lot of big talk about having a customer-first mentality but being customer centric means going beyond marketing slogans and PR campaigns - it's making customer centricity a part of how you operate.

It starts with talking to a customer in their language because there is an understanding of how they talk and think about their problems and challenges. It's putting them first so that instead of the narrative being "our company does this…" it's "we know these are the challenges you face, and these are the things keeping you up at night and we can help you solve them." It's making your product names something that telegraphs how they solve problems and when you write your marketing copy, you don't start with your company name.

Voice presents an amazing opportunity to walk the walk of being customer centric for businesses and brands. However, as voice is maturing, it's becoming more important to move from focusing on "seeing if we can" and focusing on "how to make it better." To do that requires strategic thinking throughout the process.

This book was written to help businesses, marketers, user experience professionals, and the Voice community understand the full opportunity of Voice and provide a way to take advantage of that opportunity in a way that works for their audiences and brands. We have taken all that we have learned from decades of strategically leading clients through major shifts in technology and user behavior and combined that with all that we have learned from our immersion in Voice.

While we see the potential and the opportunities that Voice

will enable, we also know how critical it is to get Voice experiences "right" so that all that potential can be realized. Our goal for this book is to help businesses and brands with the "getting it right" part and provide a place to start.

A note about a few reference items: For purposes of sanity as well as currency, we chose not to include many data points in this book. Part of this is because in the year we have been sharing and presenting data, we have had to issue updates countless times and the other part is that while it's important to have your data points at the ready to build the business case, original research about your customer is more important. We do mention some figures, so we have included a Works Cited page as well as a Works Consulted page to acknowledge all of the experts whose articles, research, and books have guided our thinking.

Ready? let's dive in!

Susan & Scot Westwater

November 22, 2019

WHAT IS VOICE
AND WHY DOES IT MATTER?

CHAPTER 1

WHAT IS VOICE?

By now, you probably have heard of smart speakers like Amazon Alexa or Google Home, but aren't quite sure what all the fuss is about and how you can use this new channel for your brand. Just as the mobile revolution changed how audiences interact with our brands and content, smart speakers are poised to do the same but with far more reaching consequences.

When we talk about Voice we are referring to any interaction that allows you to control a computer device using natural language. It could be something as basic as a TV remote with voice enhancement. It could be the Google Assistant or Apple's Siri on your smartphone. Or, it could be a new class of devices referred to as smart speakers like Amazon Alexa, Google Home, or Apple Home Pod. Voice can even be Apple's CarPlay, Google's Android Auto or any other in-car assistant. Voice really is as an umbrella term for the entire universe where voice, not a keyboard, is the main input that drives the experience.

Voice represents the first new consumer channel for marketers to reach their audience since the advent of smartphones. As with all new platforms, there are new considerations you need to keep in mind when using them to reach your audience. Voice is not radio or TV and :30-second commercials won't work because of the interactive nature of Voice. Besides, your audience expects to be able to do more than to sit and listen to commercials on these new devices.

Even in these early days of voice assistants and smart speakers, we're already seeing data that indicates the beginnings of behaviors (product research, price comparison, and purchase) that are common on other more mature platforms.

The emergence of Voice is the fourth major shift in consumer behavior in the past 30 years. The first was the shift to computers and the web in the mid to late 90s. Next was social media with Facebook and Twitter capturing a large amount of consumer attention in 2007 and 2008.

More recently, the explosion of mobile fundamentally changed how we create and consume content. More importantly, it created a new marketing channel and changed consumer purchase behavior.

Voice is poised to become the first point of contact for consumer attention. Instead of competing for eyeballs, marketers and advertisers will be competing for their ears. The best part is, it's already well under way.

CHAPTER 2

WHAT MAKES VOICE COMPELLING TO YOUR AUDIENCE?

There are many aspects of Voice that make it compelling to users and those aspects are aiding adoption at unsurpassed rates. First and foremost, voice-based devices are simply easier for most people to use. For the first time ever you can use natural language to control a computer or device. There are no special commands or visual interfaces to learn. You need only make a request and you'll get a response.

It is also much faster to speak than it is to type. The average person can type at 40-65 words per minute (WPM) while that same person can speak 120-140 WPM.

Another big benefit of Voice is that it's hands-free so users can be doing something else while using it. That ability to multitask appeals to consumers as well as professionals such as a surgeons. It's not just appealing because it works when your hands are busy and unable to swipe, tap, or click, but also because there's a reduction of friction that just makes many tasks easier.

Voice experiences can deliver a wealth in meaning where the expression or inflection in the tone of the voice informs the listener or user whether something's humorous, serious, et cetera. This gives a whole new level of tonality and in communication because voice and tone are actual literal things.

Voice is also inclusive on many levels. It empowers people who have physical limitations such as Rheumatoid Arthritis or vision impairment as well as those who have limited or no literacy. If you know how to speak and how to listen, then you can use a voice enabled device. There is also a lower price to entry than previous technology shifts as many people can use Voice on their existing smartphones or on low cost smart speaker devices. Gone are a lot of the challenges of setting up a computer and learning how to use a keyboard and/or mouse as all of those different pieces of hardware fall away.

Finally, there are entire populations who don't speak English as their primary language that will benefit from voice technology. Most websites have information in English and maybe a few pages of Spanish content but very few other if any, other languages. Voice has the potential to provide information to the groups that have been vastly under-served in the past because of language barriers.

All of this is a big opportunity for you to reach a wider audience and provide more value to more people.

CHAPTER 3

TYPES OF VOICE EXPERIENCES & DEVICES

Voice experiences can vary but there are really 3 main categories into which they fall.

Voice Only: Experiences that have voice as the only input and output. Amazon Echo Dot and Google Home are generally considered voice only although technically they are not because of their small visual cues (like the light ring on the Echo Dot).

Voice First: Instances where voice is the primary input and output but it is not the only input. Examples would be Amazon Show and Google Nest Hub.

Voice-Added: In these experiences, voice is not the primary method for input or output but instead is used as an option for assisting with input. Voice to text on mobile is a common example of this.

At this point, we'd be remiss if we didn't mention the devices that are commonly used to access these Voice experiences:

Smart speakers: Internet-enabled speaker by which a user can engage a voice assistant by spoken commands and is capable of streaming audio content, relaying information, and communicating with other devices. Examples: Google Nest Mini, Apple HomePod, Amazon Alexa Echo, Amazon Alexa Auto

Smartphones: Mobile phones that have strong hardware capabilities and extensive mobile operating systems to enable access to voice assistants. Apple's Siri, Google Assistant, Samsung's Bixby, and Amazon Alexa all have versions available for various smartphone platforms.

Additionally, iOS and Android apps can include Voice interactions to enhance and/or simplify the user experience.

Smart display: These devices are smart speakers with a touchscreen. These are one of the key drivers of the concept of multi-modal experiences where voice works in concert with visual display. Example: Amazon Alexa Show and Google Home Hub

Hearables: In-ear devices that deliver voice experiences without any screen. Examples: Apple AirPods, Amazon Earbuds, Samsung Galaxy Buds, and Google's Pixel Buds

Wearables: Similar to hearables, these devices deliver voice experiences with or without a screen but are worn on the user (not in-ear). Examples: Apple Watch, Amazon Ring

In-Auto: These are the devices that bring Voice driven experiences into automobiles. Examples: Apple CarPlay, Amazon Alexa Echo Auto, and Google's Android Auto

CHAPTER 4

WHO ARE THE MAIN PLAYERS RIGHT NOW IN THE US?

In the U.S., Amazon and Google are the dominant players with their Alexa and Google Home platforms being the most frequently purchased. That's not to say there are only two companies making these kinds of devices. Apple, Samsung, Microsoft, Facebook and a few players in the international market (like Alibaba's AliGenie or Baidu's DuerOS) have voice enabled devices available but none have attained the level of commercial success that Amazon has seen to date.

While these technology companies each have voice assistants they have taken a markedly different approach to the voice space as a whole.

Microsoft has been developing its voice assistant platform Cortana with a focus on enterprise-level engagement. Microsoft is working on quite a bit of AI enablement in their enterprise tools and Cortana's going to be their voice assistant for that.

Amazon Alexa has looked to drive mass consumer adoption from a two-pronged approach that focuses on developer outreach and templating (called blueprints) to drive voice application creation on their platform while also investing in device development. Many would argue the focus on quantity of voice apps developed has not necessarily meant quality.

Google took a more conservative approach and provided developer information but did not offer the "anyone can make one" avenues that Amazon did. They also seem to be focused on their assistant more in terms of their search product. Google has recently announced they will be indexing podcasts and Frequently Asked Questions (FAQ) pages on websites. This is in addition to Google's BERT update to the Google search algorithm which is designed to provide better results using Natural Language Processing.

Samsung already had an existing assistant in Bixby, there was yet another approach involving almost a re-launch of Bixby and concerted developer outreach to prove lessons had been learned and improvements had been made.

Apple's way forward is not as clear although some regard Siri as the pivotal first voice assistant. While Apple hasn't shared much about its vision and plans for Voice, the AirPods Pro release does indicate that Apple does have the voice first world on its radar.

CHAPTER 5

CONSUMER ADOPTION IS RECORD BREAKING

It is estimated that by 2020 anywhere from 50% - 75% of all U.S. homes will have at least one smart speaker. Depending on what day of the week it is and what publication you're reading, there's already between 90 and 140 million of these devices in U.S. homes right now. One thing to note, this number surely includes homes that have multiple devices.

When we look at how quickly these devices have been adopted by consumers, it's record-breaking. Smart speaker growth is happening faster than any other technology in the history of humankind. It took almost 10 years for smartphones to reach 50% market penetration, it's expected with smart speakers to happen within five. To put that into context, it took 10 years to reach that point with the television while radio, Internet, and computers took around 20 years[1].

In the United States, we're now are firmly in the early majority phase of adoption. That means we've moved beyond the innovators, bleeding edge folks, and even early adopters. Now we're actually starting to see the vast majority of Americans adopting these devices.

Other countries like the UK, Germany, Australia, and a few others are about nine to twelve months behind us. We always joke with our European counterparts that the U.S. will make a lot of the mistakes they will be able learn from those and actually move things ahead a lot quicker (which always gets a nice chuckle).

On top these record-breaking adoption rates, what's also really exciting is that adoption and usage is not limited to one singular age group. The usage of voice assistants happens across almost all adults starting with the younger age groups and carrying through to the older populations.

This is exciting because that gives us a lot of opportunities that we don't normally get when we're developing a new technology. It opens up the possibilities to create experiences that benefit multiple age groups instead of just the younger ones – and that's exciting.

CHAPTER 6

HOW CONSUMERS ARE USING VOICE

As we start to consider the problems and types of needs users will have from voice experiences, we are starting to see distinct usage patterns that help us understand what people doing on these devices. There are basically five categories of smart speaker users[2]:

There are the **audio listeners**, which is the natural entry point with smart speakers. Their initial usage starts with "I'm going to listen to podcasts" and/or "I'm going to listen to music."

Then there are the **inquirers** who are the folks asking questions and seeking out information. It could be something as simple as the weather and the news, but they're basically starting to use the interactive quality of the speakers.

Shoppers are users who essentially are doing their product or service research via voice devices.

Smart home control users are those who are automating their homes and enabling voice control of household items. This group has grown as has the investment Amazon has made into devices that aid with smart home automation.

For us, smart home controls have been a game changer, especially living in a cold winter climate and having holiday light decorations. The convenience of not having to climb out of bed to make sure the light timer is working or that we didn't forget to switch something off has been a great win.

And finally, there are **buyers**, who are different than a shopper because buyers are those who not only are shopping, but for sure are making a purchase.

CHAPTER 7

VOICE IS CHANGING SEARCH BEHAVIOR

Now all these adoption and usage figures sound fine and dandy, but the big mass adoption movement will be happening in 2020 and beyond. That said, we know that Voice has already had a major impact on search behavior.

When we say search, we not only mean search from a content standpoint on your website or digital entities, but also search via voice assistant and smart speakers themselves.

In 2016, Google announced 20% of the traffic that was coming to their mobile app on Android was happening via voice search. The interesting thing about that is back in

2016, voice search was still relatively new and yet we saw a large amount of people using it. Google hasn't released updated numbers but there's a strong possibility that three years later, the number has climbed to nearly 50%. The important thing to note is that even early on there was double-digit use of voice search on Android.

More recently, Microsoft shared that 25% of desktop searches on Windows 10 were actually happening via voice. It seems that as people became comfortable and familiar using voice search on mobile devices, they're trying it on their desktop.

Another significant data point is that right now 40% of adults use voice search every single day. That could be via smart speaker, smartphone, desktop, or some other device. But the point is, they're actually using it to find information that they're seeking.

It's estimated that over 260 billion web searches in the U.S. will occur via voice in 2019[3]. While this is a massive number, it will equate to 13% - 15% of all searches in the U.S.

Voice search attribution has not yet been perfected by Google, so while we don't know exact figures, the amount of Voice searches is going to climb quickly as the adoption of smart speakers and other voice enabled devices increases.

THE BUSINESS OPPORTUNITY OF VOICE

CHAPTER 8

BUSINESS INVESTMENT HASN'T CAUGHT UP WITH ADOPTION...YET

While we have all this compelling adoption data, the biggest challenge right now is business investment hasn't caught up with the consumer adoption of Voice. So, on one hand, you have the adoption of these devices among consumers, but on the other hand, you don't have a ton of content that's actually available on these platforms yet.

This creates a gap and a massive opportunity for the businesses that act now. This is where you have the potential for growth and a chance to make some inroads in a white space where your competitors aren't playing – yet.

eMarketer shared survey results that indicated 30% of senior business decision makers plan on making an investment in Voice in some capacity in 2019. In 2020, that figure actually goes up to about 62%[4].

While there may not be a lot of investment happening right now, businesses have Voice on their radar. It's something they are thinking about and many are trying to figure out how Voice can be used to deliver a better customer experience.

We know customer experience has become a really important topic because we now understand that it isn't just marketing by itself. It isn't just product or the customer service either, but rather it's everything working together. And it's a critical factor of success in today's marketing landscape.

Voice interfaces are definitely on the radar as something that is already used or is anticipated to be used to improve customer experience. So, it's coming. It's a matter of getting ahead of that wave by doing something now. This could be seen as a situation similar to those who invested early on with social media.

It's like knowing mobile was going to explode nine to twelve months before it actually happened. It's like knowing the commercial web was going to change business forever.

Consider this your fair warning!

Scot had an experience early in his career that really illustrates the hazard of businesses maintaining the status quo despite clear consumer trends. "Why are you wasting your time with the Internet? It's just a fad - it's never going to last. Print is your bread and butter – it's never going away." This was a real conversation Scot had with a Creative Director very early on in his career. The year was 1998 or 1999, he can't even remember at this point.

Print and other traditional marketing tactics were the order of the day. The Internet was brand new and a lot of people were uncomfortable using it let alone marketing their products with it.

Back in those days, there weren't online classes or videos you could watch. You had to learn by doing and that's exactly what he did. It was a lot of the early experimentation that led to Scot's deep love of the intersection of technology and art.

As digital projects would come up at his first agency, he would volunteer his time just to get a crack at them. He'd work nights and weekends to have the opportunity to get some digital chops and gain experience. At this point, there weren't years of best practices and knowledge to draw from so the team was making it up as they went along (usability and information architecture really weren't mainstays of digital design yet).

All these years later, he still remembers the conversation he had with that Creative Director and is reminded of it every time someone wants to stick with the status quo.

As we mentioned earlier, this is actually the third major shift we've seen in technology (fourth, if you include social media) during the course of our careers and the pattern is pretty well defined. Yet we keep hearing the same story over and over again:

No one will ever buy anything on the Internet. They'll never put their credit card into a website. Now we have Amazon and other online only retailers that sell more product than physical stores. We also have Cyber Monday to take advantage of all the U.S.. shoppers who do their Q4 Holiday purchases on the web.

No one will ever buy anything on a smartphone. There's no way anyone will ever put a credit card into their smartphone. Now we have Apple Pay and Google Pay plus countless other ways to make purchases and send money to each other from our phones.

No one will ever buy anything off of social media. There's no way anyone will make purchases using social and yet ever day millions of dollars worth of products are sold from Instagram and Facebook.

No one will ever buy anything with Voice. We are already hearing the same exact thing that we've heard about the other technologies. The funny thing is, we actually have the data that shows people are already making purchases with their smart speakers. This trend is only going to grow (more on that later).

For those of you that have been around for the past 10 years, this is exactly like the early days of mobile and responsive design. Initially it was difficult to convince clients that investing in mobile optimized experiences was worth their time (and budget). Even as late as 2014, we were still having conversations about why mobile optimized experiences were necessary. A lot of businesses adopted a wait-and-see approach on mobile – and they got burned.

With Voice the stakes are even greater, especially when you consider voice search. In the next few years, having voice optimized content is going to be as basic as having a

website or social media presence. Voice is going to become

a non-negotiable for consumers very, very quickly.

CHAPTER 9

WHAT MAKES VOICE COMPELLING TO BUSINESSES?

We spend most of our time talking to businesses, entrepreneurs, marketers, and the thing on everyone's mind is really "what's in it for me?" They want to know why they should pay attention to Voice and how it can either increase revenue or reduce cost.

Voice offers up a whole new way to reach and engage with your entire audience. It's the first new channel since mobile and it has the potential for inclusivity and accessibility that brands haven't previously experienced.

Much like a website, voice assistants are available 24 hours a day, 7 days a week, 365 days a year. There's no such thing as a holiday or a day off so they are always there to answer questions and assist your customers. Unlike a human operator, they can also have hundreds upon hundreds of conversations at the same time without needing to scale up resources.

Voice also allows you to create a new dimension for your brand. The concept of voice and tone become literal and not just figurative ideas for copy and design. Your brand now has an actual sound and quite possibly its own distinct voice. Its persona is now the personality that creates the character your audiences speak to and engage with, creating an even more robust experience and emotional connection.

Voice also provides a new avenue for creating good customer experiences. As mentioned earlier, there's the 24/7 support where it can provide information and help with simple tasks without looking up a phone number, waiting on hold, or searching a website. A good experience from a customer perspective allows them to get what they want when they want it.

Voice can also provide another way for your customers to use your product. A great example is how Comcast now provides the Xfinity remote which is voice-enabled. Extensions like that can enhance the customer experience without requiring a complete reinvention or entirely new product features. There's an opportunity to leverage what your brand is doing well or delivering and provide that value in a whole different way.

From a business perspective, you're able to deliver a good experience that allows businesses to deliver on customer expectations, have 24/7 availability, and prove true customer centricity because in the voice space you have to lead with what it is your customer needs. No one wants to hear a 20-minute monologue about your brand. You have to provide the information and answers they want and need. And so you walk that walk of being customer led. Voice enables constant availability without compromising quality because it isn't about increasing staff, it's just about using your content and making it available in all the right places and all the right mediums.

Voice can improve efficiency to reduce costs and increase revenue. But if applied thoughtfully with your customers in mind, Voice can be used to not only reduce costs internally, but potentially even increase revenue over time by creating a better customer experience.

Consider this: According to IBM, US companies spend close to 1.3 trillion dollars annually on customer support through call centers[5]. If you were able to offload 1% of those calls to a voice assistant or chatbot, the reduction in calls would save 13 billion dollars per year.

CHAPTER 10

INTRODUCING THE VOICE WEB

For those of you who have been around the web for a while, you will remember that search engine optimization (SEO) wasn't a thing at first. We didn't know about it until after we had built so many websites and generated so much content that users needed help finding what they were looking for.

With the advent of search engines, SEO became critical for your website to get discovered. So we had ranking factors. When mobile devices started hitting the consumer market, the initial thought was "Oh well we don't have to worry about mobile. No one's using that." It wasn't long before Google started making ranking factors specifically for mobile. Now, it's essentially a ranking requirement to have mobile optimized experiences. It's not too far a stretch to imagine that while right now voice isn't necessarily part of the consideration set for ranking, Google and other search engines eventually start to increase the ranking factors around voice content because of the shift in behavior we are starting to see now.

With that shift in behavior, there will need to be a shift in your SEO strategy. If you're familiar with websites and how to optimize content for the web, the predominant strategy focuses on keywords: single words, multiple word phrases, and short pieces like that. The goal was to optimize your web pages and content against those words so that when someone typed in a single word or those couple words, your website or web page showed up on the first page of search results (preferably at the top).

With speech and natural language, though, instead of asking for a car, we start asking in full phrases and full questions because that is how humans naturally ask questions.

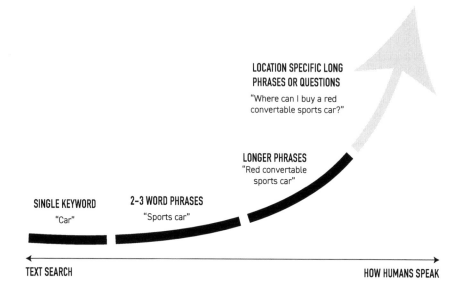

Fig. 10.1 Illustration showing the progression from single keyword to longtail phrase in SEO

We start having additional context and descriptors so it's a lot richer question. What used to be "new convertible car" evolves into:

Where can I buy a new convertible car?

Where can I buy a sports car around me?

Where can I buy a red convertible car near me?

"How do I…" is also something that commonly appears at the beginning of these queries. If there's only one thing that you take away from this entire book (we honestly hope it's a lot more), it's that you need to start optimizing your website right now.

Only one-third of all websites are actually optimized for these longer tail phrases which leaves a lot of room for opportunity. That's going to benefit you not only from a traditional web search perspective, but it's also a way you can start to prepare as we start moving more and more into voice search.

Google recently made an update to their search algorithm which they've called BERT (an acronym for Bidirectional Encoder Representations from Transformers). BERT uses Natural Language Processing (NLP) to consider the context of the words in a search query. The goal is to provide better search results and answers to person looking for it. Initially it will impact 1 in 10 searches in the US but will expand its reach over time.

When it comes to Amazon Alexa, it's critical to know that when you ask a question, there are three places it looks to for an answer. We visualize the way Alexa seeks an answer similar to the rings of a tree.

The innermost ring is Alexa's own database of information which is checked first for the answer. Basic queries like weather, traffic or sports scores are examples of the types of questions that will be answered via that "first search" ring.

Fig. 10.2 Illustration of how voice search works on Amazon Alexa

If the device doesn't find the answer internally, it looks out to a second "ring" which we refer to as the "Voice Web."

In that ring, Alexa is widening the search to include any apps or skills to find the answer. As it continues its search, it is essentially reviewing the content in a similar manner to a search engine:

Is this content from a credible skill?

Has it been updated recently?

Are people coming back to it?

And a bunch of other ranking factors, quite frankly, we just don't know yet.

If an answer to the question exists in the "Voice Web" and it meets all these different criteria, that's the answer that Alexa gives.

Let that sink in for a moment. If someone asks a question and the answer is in the "Voice Web" Alexa never looks at content on the general Internet. With smart speakers you don't get a page full of blue links when you ask a question.

It's one question, one answer.

Over time, this could have a serious impact on organic web traffic. If it does have a negative impact, wouldn't you rather your audience find your voice content instead of your competitors? In the new world of voice search, whomever provides the best answer to your audience's questions wins.

If Alexa doesn't find the answer on the "Voice Web," it opens up the search to the widest "ring": the general Internet. At that moment, the quest for the answer becomes a long tail web search. If you're using a Google Assistant, obviously Google is the search engine but if you're using Alexa, it's using Bing. Google voice devices work similarly to Alexa but recently Google announced that it would be including podcast and Frequently Asked Questions page content as part of the "Voice web."

If your content is not optimized for voice search or long tail keywords, it's likely the voice assistants won't find any of your content. In those instances, what will be found and served is either coming from Wikipedia or Yelp.

That is a scary proposition for a lot of people that we talk to, brand managers especially. Often when we explain that the voice search content about their brand is coming from Wikipedia, they often respond "Wait, I've spent $100 million building my brand. What do you mean Wikipedia is the answer when someone asks about my brand?" As an experiment, if you have a smartphone or smart speaker, ask Alexa or Google Assistant about any brand you can think of and see what answer is provided and its source. You'll be surprised at how many brands aren't accounting for voice search yet.

The default to Wikipedia or Yelp isn't some sort of conspiracy to unseat established brands. Quite simply, Amazon and Google both want to provide some sort of an answer. So, if the assistant can't find your content, it will use those other sources because any answer is better than giving no answer. There isn't much tolerance for "I'm sorry. I don't know the answer to that" before a user stops using their assistant so it's a matter of survival.

CHAPTER 11

WHY YOU NEED TO START OPTIMIZING FOR VOICE SEARCH RIGHT NOW

Many marketers and businesses seem to be waiting for the "killer voice app" before investing heavily in Voice. While voice search isn't necessarily an "app", it's definitely driving a lot traffic and should not be overlooked.

Eventually, when someone asks Alexa or Google Assistant a question relevant to your industry, if you've done the work needed to optimize for voice search, your answer will be the one provided.

By investing in Voice now, a #2 or #3 player will have the ability to outrank the #1 player on the web in their industry.

Creating voice content in a skill is also the only content you can truly control in the Alexa universe. Having your Wikipedia page updated right now helps when someone asks about your brand but, remember, no brand truly controls its Wikipedia page.

Looking a few years down the road as voice search becomes more prevalent and the amount of voice only content available grows, web search marketing will become secondary. The key is to start now to own the answers for your industry before your competition does.

There are ways you can optimize your website, and quite frankly, a lot of SEO best practices still apply, especially if you're focusing on long tail search queries. If you're in the "answer box" or "knowledge graph" that shows up on Google Search Results pages, you have a very high chance of actually being returned as the number one web result and a high likelihood of being the answer on Google Assistant.

Achieving that requires you to optimize your website by

applying current SEO best practices. So start with investing in search, because over time, you'll have the ability to own the answers for your industry or category.

Then focus on your voice content. It can be as basic as providing answers to different questions relevant to your brand and how its products are used (we will get deeper on what that content should be later). As you drive your audience to use the voice skill to get their information, over time your answers are going to start to become the credible answer on the Voice Web.

Because of the way the assistants seek out answers, the general web organic search rank won't be as critical if the questions are being answered before it's necessary to look there. This means you can effectively own the answers for your entire category – provided you develop the content for the questions – which is an incredibly powerful position.

As a result of this, we really need to start thinking about a skill or an action as the new website and you need to have content within these experiences that your audience is looking for. That makes it imperative to understand the types of questions your audience has, what their struggles are, and actually how your brand solves those problems.

CHAPTER 12

VOICE COMMERCE IS COMING

Lastly, Voice commerce (also referred to as v-commerce or v-com) is estimated to be an $80 billion proposition by 2023. Amazon has even predicted that Voice will account for $40 billion as soon as next year.

V-com is estimated to be around 1.3 billion dollars worth of sales right now, so there's an incredible amount of growth expected to happen over the next 3-4 years. These predictions also shows how ubiquitous this is medium is anticipated to become.

When you look at Voice usage data, you do see the beginnings of a customer journey playing out. You see that people are using voice assistants to do product research and price comparison. There is a lot of activity happening during the awareness and consideration phases of the journey.

As you look deeper into the data you start to see behaviors typically associated with purchase - store lookup, placing orders, checking order status, and even reordering frequently purchased items. While it's in its infancy, voice commerce is already starting to show up in the data and it's going to only continue to grow.

If you're selling any sort of product online and you're doing e-commerce, you can't really afford to ignore this trend. Start looking at ways you can optimize not only your website, but also start creating voice experiences as well. That way when people are ready to start buying in mass, you have something somewhere for them to go. Because you certainly don't want them to go to your competitors.

SECTION 3

THE IMPORTANCE OF BEING
USEFUL AND USABLE

CHAPTER 13

WHAT IT MEANS TO BE USEFUL AND USABLE

Regardless of delivery channel, the goal should always be to deliver useful and usable information to our audiences.

Useful is what gives content value to a target audience because it either meets a need or helps complete a task.

Usable refers to being easily understood, navigated and actually used.

Both are critical for a successful & valuable voice experience. In reality, both are critical for almost all aspects of content and customer experience.

An audience really just wants us to solve their problem or make their tasks easier. They don't care about the technology, improving customer experience, decreasing cost, and all that stuff. What they really want to know is how does this business or product solve their problem?

Because we all know what happens if we actually don't solve real customer problems: we become part of the perceived problem. And that results in a lot of angry emojis, tweets, phone calls, and a lot of push back and negative press from your audience.

There has been a trend towards businesses becoming more customer centric or at least customer driven. How do you do that you ask? It's simple. You start with your customer and their needs, challenges, and pain points to inform your content across all mediums.

This enables you to deliver the right message to the right person at the right time. When you start with what your customer needs and then move progressively through the different areas and channels that they would use as touch points, you are able to create consistent content and messaging that resonates with them. Those messages are also amplified because they are reinforced versus redefined at every touch point. It also puts your customer in the driver's seat so they can start from their preferred area and continue through their preferred mode of interaction.

Solving customer problems sounds easy, right? After all, we know the technology, we know our brand, we know our category, etc. But more often than not, we don't really have a clear view of our audience or what their top tasks and challenges are.

It's important we know that though, because when a business understands what their audience needs, it can see where the overlaps are with its own business objectives. It's at that intersection of need and objective where there is an opportunity to deliver value (and to be useful).

FOCUS YOUR EFFORTS HERE

Fig 13.1 Illustration of the intersection of audience needs and business objectives which is the key to strategic success.

You really want to figure out what your audience needs are, what your business objectives are, and where they overlap so you can focus your efforts in the right areas. In order to ensure success or a higher level of success and certainty, you really need to know what your audience needs out of the experience. You also need to understand what you're trying to achieve with the experience for your brand. Is it lead generation? Is it a sale? Is it actually customer support after purchase? These are all very viable ways to leverage Voice, but you really need to figure out where it makes the most sense and can have the biggest amount of impact for your customers.

CHAPTER 14

VOICE FIRST = CUSTOMER FIRST

This is why, in our minds, Voice First equals Customer First from a user experience and content perspective. When we talk about customer first, what we mean is a customer's information needs and tasks don't change regardless of how they access that information. Their interaction may change based on the device they are using, but what they're trying to accomplish is the same. They still need to complete the same tasks and they still need to answer the same questions.

Working with Voice as your first touch point is a very demanding way to start thinking about exactly what your customer needs because voice does not leave much leeway for talking about yourself and for not serving your user. If you think about conversations, anyone who talks about themselves too long is someone you probably won't seek out for help or information. So, if you want to be successful, you have to keep the customer at the center of every interaction.

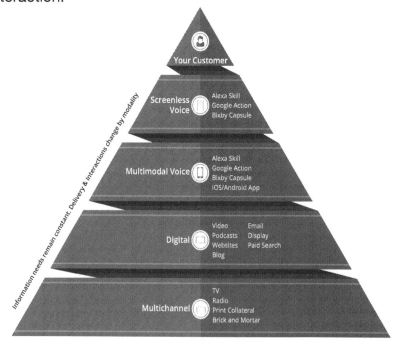

Fig 14.1 Illustration of a customer centric approach to content

We also start with Voice because we already are seeing statistics showing that Voice is going to be the first touch point for consumers because of its ease of use and the compelling characteristics that we discussed earlier.

After that first touch, our customer may start to interact with all of the other channels that exist depending upon their preference or need. They could also continue on a path that is primarily Voice driven.

Regardless of how a user navigates the entire experience, the reality is that what channels are included in their total brand experience are based on their own choice and preference. It's our job then to make sure we are able to always address their needs across the various touch points and channels consistently.

Another reason we start with voice only is because, from a practicality and execution standpoint, voice only is the hardest content delivery experience to solve for because there are no visuals to lean on. There's no screens and no additional visual context. As a result, you have to rely on the voice performance and the content to actually answer the question and guide the user to the next step or task.

What we learned from mobile first design is that it's much easier to add to an experience than take away from it. As a result, we've adapted the idea of progressive enhancement for voice experiences. As devices get progressively more capable (processor-wise or screen wise) you can add things that expand experiences like additional images, animations, videos, etc. It's not just limited to digital though so you can take that all the way through to video, television, and even in-store. But the idea is you're starting with the customer at the very core and trying to fulfill their needs all the way through all of your content and all of your messaging.

In the spirit of that approach, start with voice only first. Once that experience is really nailed down, then enhance the experience by adding visuals to it for multi modal devices like the Amazon Echo Show. It's also a good idea to think about how your voice experience works on a smartphone since voice assistants are used on those devices as well.

CHAPTER 15

STARTING SMALL

We are big proponents of starting small and evolving the experience over time as you learn how your audience is using a voice application. Voice is a new channel so driving discovery and teaching users to use your voice applications is going to take a bit of time and support. It's helpful to start small so you can deliver on your promise of being useful and usable and building trust (as well as usage).

Developing a voice experience also does not necessarily mean reinventing the wheel when it comes to content. Most brands have a significant library of content they can leverage for initial voice applications. It's not just being efficient; it's setting a path for consistent messages and branding.

SUSAN & SCOT WESTWATER

When we talk about use cases, there are a few basic approaches we can consider from the start. In North America, we see a lot of question and answer types of experiences. To date, it's been very much a crawl, walk, run approach.

One thing we often talk with brands about is getting their product and company information out on the Voice Web for their audiences. This is important in the context of search because it lays down a foundation of information on the Voice Web. Getting your information out on the Voice Web gives greater control over what answers are being returned when someone searches for your product and brand. But that doesn't mean you should just put information out there as long monologues. It has to be done in a thoughtful and relevant manner.

You need to present information in relation to the questions and information needs of your users. Depending on the phase of the customer journey, this could be questions asked while a prospective customer is doing research so they can make a purchase decision. Or perhaps it's after someone has purchased your product and has questions that would normally be routed to a call center.

VOICE USE CASE THOUGHT STARTERS

If there are simple things that can be done without the aid of a human, those things can be managed via Voice. That frees up your actual call center representatives to handle the complex problems that your customer might have.

Direct to consumer flash briefings with a "tip of the day" are a great way of getting into someone's daily routine and giving your brand an opportunity to become a part of someone's life.

Another use case applies to internal communications and information for companies that either goes ignored in an email or is buried on the company intranet. Publicly accessible information such as company holidays, key dates like open enrollment, or even the IT Help Desk's contact information can be used to answer employee questions like "Do I have President's Day off?" easily and quickly. Flash Briefings can also be used for company news and notices.

Here are a few additional examples of some Voice experiences that demonstrate how you can leverage existing content, help customer service, and improve your operational efficiency.

Tide Stain Remover Skill: This Amazon Alexa skill's purpose is to answer 200 different questions about removing stains and doing laundry. It seems quite basic but it solves a problem that many college freshmen and others face the first time they are doing laundry on their own. Basically, Tide is helping solve a user problem with existing content that now is available via Alexa.

Right now, it's an informational skill but it isn't a big stretch to believe that in the future that skill could include coupons or offer up in-skill purchase (Hey, if you want to buy this product...). So, this skill is Tide building a foundation in its category on the Voice Web by getting a lot of useful information out into the universe and having people know, like, and trust them so that they can, over time, add features like v-commerce to it for revenue.

Send Me a Sample: This is another Alexa skill but instead of being tied to a single brand, it's an app where a user can request product samples to be sent directly to them. It's an interesting example because the skill is the actual marketing tactic versus a sampling tactic that has been added to another skill. Now the skill does require some online registration for set up but once that is complete, it's a matter of asking for a sample. When we tried it, the skill told us it had samples of Nutella and asked if we wanted them. We replied yes and three weeks later, we received a package with Nutella samples.

Having managed our share of in-store sampling programs during our careers, we see a lot of efficiency with this process. Not only are you able to reduce waste because it's on-demand, you also get visibility into who actually wants to try your product and have new leads for marketing. You also are not relying on someone in-store to remember what to say about your product or brand. That is handled in the skill with your content so it's consistent. For the consumer, they are getting samples of a product they want without even leaving the house.

Butterball Turkey Hot line: For the past 30 years, Butterball Turkey has had a "turkey hot line" during the Thanksgiving holiday in the U.S. Thanksgiving is usually one of the first big holidays that either a new couple or homeowner usually hosts. It's a big meal and all friends and family are invited. So, if you don't have a lot of experience cooking, it's an incredibly stressful event. Thanksgiving dinner also has many emotions and nostalgia tied to it that make it even more emotionally charged.

The traditional main course is a whole turkey so Butterball recognized the opportunity to help and provide this hot line to field common questions from frazzled people trying to make Thanksgiving dinner. So last year they actually had three of their operators record themselves speaking the answers they would commonly give. It might be Ruthie who tells you the ideal cooking temperature for a turkey or Christopher who helps you figure out how large a turkey you need for 20 people. All of this and more is just a skill and a question away. No need to call and wait on hold, simply ask your turkey question to your Alexa device and you can just go on with your day.

The content for the skill came from all of the previous call scripts so there was consistency with the phone experience too. The chef or cook's questions didn't change so there wasn't a need to change the information. But the interaction did change so the effort came in making the conversations flow well. Butterball didn't reinvent the wheel, they simply made it run more smoothly.

HOW TO GET STARTED WITH CREATING VALUABLE EXPERIENCES

CHAPTER 16

CRAWL, WALK, RUN

When it comes to Voice, starting simple is not necessarily starting small if you are solving a big problem for your audience. The first lesson when starting out is to keep it simple. Then start to build and iterate based on what you learn from actual usage.

A "crawl, walk, run" approach works well in this space because it enables a brand to enter the space while having enough flexibility to adjust as the Voice channel evolves. It also makes it possible for developing a proof of concept with a clear objective.

Taking an iterative approach also builds in an important

aspect of the plan which is continued optimization and iteration. As with all digital content, "launching and leaving" a voice experience is a bad practice. There are many ways to utilize Voice but just launching something and then walking away is definitely not one of the right ones. So, when you make that decision to design and implement a voice experience, know that you should have a road map and a plan that will extend well beyond launch.

CHAPTER 17

A FAMILIAR PROCESS FOR A NOT SO FAMILIAR CHANNEL

Another thing our clients often ask about is our process or workflow. It helps them understand the effort and also how things will happen. It also assures them we have a "plan" and know what we're doing.

That said, we've established a process for creating a voice experience. If you've done any amount of website development or audio/video production, parts of this process are going to be very familiar to you. We have taken the best of a web design/app process and combined that with audio and video production workflows. This is because there's a variety of components involved in the planning, creation and launch of a voice experience. As a result, we have this somewhat familiar but unique process that can take you from an idea to actually executing to continued optimization and improvement. We call it the Pragmatic Blueprint.

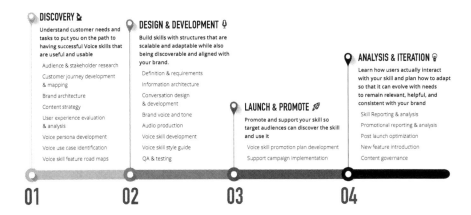

Fig 17.1 Illustration of the Pragmatic Blueprint.

1. Discovery

Understand customer needs, tasks, and business objectives to put you on the path to having successful Voice experiences that are useful and usable.

2. Design & Development

Build voice apps with structures that are scalable and adaptable while also being discoverable and aligned with your brand.

3. Launch & Promote

Promote and support your voice app so target audiences can discover the skill and use it

4. Analysis & Iteration

Learn how users actually interact with your voice app and plan how to adapt so that it can evolve with needs to remain relevant, helpful, and consistent with your brand

In the next few chapters we'll go deeper into each phase to give you a better sense of what's included and how tasks in one phase inform the next one.

Ready? Let's go!

CHAPTER 18

PHASE I: DISCOVERY

Our blueprint starts with Discovery because it's incredibly important since it sets the foundation for everything. To build a successful experience, you have to know what your audience needs, what their frustrations are, and what their challenges are, so that as a brand, you can identify how you can actually solve their problems. If you don't know that, your experience it's going to be a lot of talking at your audience versus helping them with their needs.

The Discovery phase gives us the opportunity to do our homework about our audience so we can determine how we can deliver the most value where it makes sense for the brand.

Discovery is important when developing a voice experience because, right now, we don't have many (if any) best practices within the voice space. We see this as a good thing. With the web and maybe even mobile apps, there is tendency to defer to "best practices" so we can skip the discovery process and get to market faster.

What this approach has actually done is led us down false paths and caused a lot of rework and pivoting that otherwise could be avoided. By doing that discovery work upfront, you're going to refine assumptions or confirm them through research. You're also going to learn how to reduce the cone of uncertainty.

When you start a project, you usually are starting with a problem that could be solved hundreds of ways. What you're doing during Discovery is taking the time to understand what your audience wants and needs so you can focus your effort based on real information, not assumptions. It gives you the ability zero in on the solutions that will work best based on that real information.

Discovery is also where you should conduct your stakeholder interviews to identify what the goals and objectives of the project are from a business standpoint. Don't skip this step! Spending 3-4 hours defining the project from this perspective will save you a lot of heartache and possible misunderstandings down the road.

Once you have all of this information, establish the goals to be tracked by Key Performance Indicators (KPIs) that show if the solution actually delivered on what you set out to do.

Discovery should be viewed as a non-negotiable. There's too many unknowns and assumptions at the beginning of a project. The truth is, unless we are talking to our intended audience and client stakeholders we don't have the information necessary to create a successful Voice strategy.

Let's face it without discovery in a project , you're just guessing. You're creating something that you hope actually works and spending a lot of money to find out (by the way, hope is not a strategy).

Keep in mind that Voice isn't a standalone tactic - it needs to live as a part of a larger brand ecosystem. If you have a content strategy, look at ways to leverage what already exists, especially from a content standpoint and see how you can optimize it for Voice.

If you don't have a content strategy, you certainly want to establish what you're trying to communicate to your audience so that you reach the right person with the right message at the right time. It's important that all the components of your brand experience are aligned and a cohesive content strategy can accomplish that.

During the Discovery phase of a voice project (or any type of project for that matter) it's the least expensive time to pivot. It's the best time to have to change course because there is so much flexibility left in the requirements and nothing tangible has been built yet.

So, take the time to get yourself to a point where you know that you have a solid strategy and approach. This is the perfect time to "poke holes" in your assumptions and plans because if you have to change, it's okay.

Major revisions during the Design and Development phase, or even worse at the Launch phase are going to take a lot more effort and a lot more dollars (and probably an extra explanation or two to leadership).

Discovery is the ready and aim before you start firing.

Scot has a great story that demonstrates the importance of Discovery. During his previous agency days, he had client who had come to them and said that one of their target audiences was clamoring for a specific type of information. As a result, this client wanted the agency to build a platform with this information for that audience. It was a significant project that would cost about $5 million. Now what was interesting, is that all of the data that Scot had heard up until that point that was from that audience indicated they had absolutely no interest in such a platform.

Scot did a small amount of research by talking to maybe five or six people who fit the audience profile. He basically asked them what type of things they needed and got a sense of what their day was like. As Scot conducted that research, it became very clear, very quickly that what they were going to spend $5 million on to build was completely the wrong thing.

They presented the findings to the client and as result, the entire project was completely changed. It took less than a week and a fraction of the overall project budget to uncover this information which steered the project away from what would have been the wrong thing and towards a more effective solution.

Since we're on the topic of research, let's talk about competitive reviews and research. Competitive research can seem like a good thing because you can see what your competitors are doing. But the reality is, you don't know if what they're doing is effective or not. You don't know if they took the time to talk to their customers and/or sales teams to get a true understanding of their challenges and needs. You also don't know what their goals were.

For all you know, they're in the middle of a re-branding or repositioning that they haven't released to the media yet and it's all going to change in a month. Remember, they aren't delivering against your organization's value proposition, you are. When you're looking something strategically, you don't know what decisions were made. You don't know what the internal politics of the organization were or what constraints the team was working against. You just don't know.

Our point of view is competitive research is great for inspiration, but if you are looking for product definition or guidance, you should be talking to your customers.

It's perfectly fine to look at competitors to understand how they are differentiating themselves or how they are handling things as long as you prioritize your audience feedback. Avoid the trap of thinking you should be following a competitor's lead because they're larger, have greater market share or a "cool" voice experience.

The goal of Discovery is to understand customer needs and tasks to put you on the path to having useful and usable voice experiences. You will more than likely do research, interviews, customer journey mapping and develop a variety of personas (brand, user and possibly even system). You should also come away with a real project scope along with a road map - both of which are great for estimation and project planning.

CHAPTER 19

PHASE II: DESIGN & DEVELOPMENT

Once Discovery work is completed, you can progress into the Design and Development phase. The reason this phase is called "Design and Development" is because we are firm believers that conversation design and development have to happen collaboratively. There needs to be a lot of communication between the teams. Although they are different skill sets, they need to be working together during this phase. It makes it easier to discover issues and solve them more effectively.

The Design and Development phase is more than conversation flows and actual development. Those are key parts of the work done during this phase but there are other pieces that come into play. During Discovery you identified all the things the experience is going to accomplish and what your audience needed from it. In Design and Development, we start defining that experience and building out requirements so that it's not something that is left to the imagination or assumption. This means you actually will have a "North star" that can be pointed back to and referenced, which is especially helpful if you start having scope creep or if your team members or stakeholders change. You can actually point back to this documentation and point out when something is not included in what is planned for that release or version.

As we design and develop an experience, there are three personas at play. We have our **user persona**, which is going to help us with identifying user tasks and help us understand the person who is doing them. The **brand persona** lives outside of all the channels and guides the brand as a whole. It's the core personality, the master brand style guide, and all of the manifestations that may or may not actually be a character. And then there's the **system persona** (a term coined by Heidi Culbertson), which focuses on how that brand will be extended into an actual voice and personality for your voice experience.

If your brand already has a persona, you can start to zero in on how that persona is manifested as the system persona and document it. This is when you will decide if your brand should have a singular system persona or perhaps multiple personas and voices. This is also when you should be thinking through your sonic brand system which will go beyond the voice.

If you don't have a brand persona or a sonic brand system, this is the time to develop them so you can use them not only for your voice experience, but across the entire brand experience. They can go into commercials, web content, and a host of different things.

Once you've established your various personas, you can document the elements such as tone, expression and language in a style guide. This not only records what has been decided but also makes it possible for others to understand the how the brand persona lives in the Voice channel and how the experience should sound and feel.

As you develop the system personas, think through the context and scenarios where a user will engage with them so you can create a robust personality that responds appropriately. It's also important that all these personas align with the master brand because the intended audience will expect a seamless consistency. Anything that's not consistent will be cause for pause. Remember your users do not say, "Oh, that's the web persona" or "that's the voice system persona." They expect it all to work together as one grand brand.

With our user tasks and information needs in mind, we start to map and plan to find gaps and traps in your conversation design. Don't just plan conversation flows based on the critical (or happy) path but think well beyond that path and explore the ways someone can get off of that path. In web design there is a tendency to work through happy path, which can be a very smooth and linear way that someone moves through the site. Conversations can be fairly nonlinear so you need to think about that and how you can help someone get to their end goal, even if they don't take the most direct path.

Just as you were planning and understanding your customer journey to identify tasks and needs, now you're going to be mapping and planning your conversation flow against accomplishing those tasks and fulfilling those needs.

This is where information architecture and content strategy are incredibly helpful. Not just on how content will be organized and structured, but also from the idea of connected content and the connectivity between the messages and tasks across all channels. You might look at how something is handled on the website, by customer service in-store, or in the call center script. And then determine how to translate that information into a voice experience while remaining aligned with those pieces so that you are not reinventing the wheel.

This should inform your voice style guide but also help develop an understanding of how to map and script out those experiences for Voice. We start out by asking these types of questions to shape the experience and content:

What is that ideal path?

What is necessary to include in a confirmation?

When should we include that confirmation?

How long do we wait for a response?

And so on...

We need to get into the nitty gritty details of a conversation flow so we can make sure that we don't leave anyone stranded. No one ever wants to hear "I'm sorry, I can't help you with that" or "I'm sorry I didn't understand you" more than a couple of times. So, think through how the experience will handle incorrect answers and out of bounds requests. We need to think through how we get the user back to their path as well as identifying when it is appropriate direct them to a human to contact for help.

It's not a failure to hand off but, it is a matter of planning that through to avoid feeling like one. With planning, we can work through the experiences so that errors remain controlled and don't make the experience sloppy.

When working with conversation flows, it's a really good idea to not only script it out, but also do live role plays to see if it feels like a natural conversation. Quite often, what's written on a piece of paper performs very differently and there really isn't a foolproof way to detect that without reading it aloud. You want to make sure that it actually sounds like a real conversation versus something that sounds really good or it looks really good on paper but just doesn't sound and feel authentic.

There's a lot more that goes into proper conversation and voice user interface design that we won't go into in this book, since it's focused more on the strategy fueling those important pieces of a voice experience. However, in the Work Consulted section at the end of this book, we have included a few books that provide valuable guidance and insight.

If you have chosen not to use the device voices and need to record audio responses, this is when that process also happens. During the developing of your sonic brand, there probably were discussions around the voice (or voices) but now it's time to go through casting, recording, editing and all that good stuff. Again, if you have any experience with advertising, this part may feel familiar.

Once everything starts to come together into the brilliant voice experience you have built with your team, you are close to launch. It may be tempting to skip thorough testing and QA in a desire to get to market but it's time well spent. It's far better for your team to discover the rough edges than having a user encounter them and hurting their perception of your experience.

CHAPTER 20

PHASE III: LAUNCH & PROMOTE

When we first created the blueprint, we actually only had three steps mapped out in the process. We quickly came to learn that while consumers are adopting voice enabled devices, especially smart speakers, they don't necessarily know all the ways to use them. As with any new technology, discovery and adoption of the applications requires launch plans and support to introduce and train users on why they are valuable and how to use them. So, we added the "Launch and Promote" phase to account for the planning, promotion, and support that is needed for success.

Right now, an overwhelming majority of people find out about voice experiences, specifically Alexa Skills and

Google Actions, by word of mouth referral from family and friends. There's also the "what's new" emails that come from Amazon, Google, and a few others where there is skill or action promotion along with some feature highlights. There are some people who are searching on their smart speakers or exploring via the recommendations from their smart speakers. Discoverability is an issue but it's the same issue that was seen before during the early days of the web and even the iOS and Android app stores.

Susan has a story that helps illustrate this. She was working with a major consumer packaged goods company back in the late nineties when the web was just taking the world by storm and people were learning how to use it to market and not just create simple websites. At the time, she had a senior brand manager for a very large brand who was questioning why a website was necessary and on top of that, why it would be necessary to include the URL of that website on all packaging and other marketing materials. The brand had a sizable budget so this was really a question about the viability of the web. In hindsight, it seems silly but basically the team had to fight to get a website created and then to get that URL put on packaging because they needed to use every paid, owned and earned channel to drive traffic. They had messages everywhere: use our website, go to our website, look at our website, here's what you can do on our website, etc. With that effort, we learned pretty quickly that if we didn't tell our audiences where to go and why, most wouldn't bother going there to find out for themselves.

This reality still holds true. So if you build a voice experience, they won't seek it out unless you tell them it exists and how it can help them. There needs to be a concerted effort to drive awareness and traffic to the experiences we have created. It's an important part of the process to develop a promotional plan that will make sure that your target audiences know the voice app exists and also how these tools, can help solve their problems.

To take advantage of the "news" that is your new voice

experience (this also applies to significant feature releases), have a promotional plan ready. Use a launch as a way to reach out to customers and show them you care about their experience and are actively working to improve it every day. There's a number of approaches that can be taken depending on the audiences you're reaching.

It's important to cross promote across every channel available whether it's paid (advertising), owned (websites and social properties), or earned (public relations) to drive traffic. It's not cannibalization. It's showing that your brand experience is that much more robust. You probably have a lot of different tactics where you can integrate something about your voice app.

You could create a promotional landing page, which was very common in the early days of iOS apps, with an explainer video on it, talking about what the features are and why people want to use it. Butterball actually has a video for their Turkey hot line on YouTube which does exactly that.

YouTube and other social channels are great for getting your message out, especially if you have a fairly sizable following.

If you have any sort of email lists send a special invitation to your subscribers or at a minimum include a mention your newsletter.

Include information about the voice app on your call center hold message.

Talk about it in podcasts and any other interviews you might be able to secure.

Once you've gone through all the owned and earned channels (and you have the budget available), you can look at paid search, paid social and other ways you can advertise. But really look at a holistic marketing plan to promote this so you can have sustained presence.

After launch, there should be continued support of your experience. Weave your voice app into your ecosystem by simply adding invocation prompts or information to marketing pieces and digital properties (it can as simple as adding it to an email signature). As we said before, if you build it, they're not necessarily going to come. You have to let them know your voice app exists and actually tell them why they need to start using it.

You really want to make sure that you're getting as many people in your ideal audience using your voice app. Because if people are not using it, you're not going to get the volume of data needed to justify continued investment in the experience. You're also not going to be able to show the algorithms that people are using your experience and get better rankings in the skill store.

CHAPTER 21

PHASE IV: ANALYSIS & ITERATION

The final phase is of the blueprint is Analysis and Iteration. This is really where the rubber meets the road, where you can look at what worked, what didn't, and how you can evolve your voice experience to provide more value or simply work better.

As with any interactive experience, you can't launch it and then ignore it, expecting a first release to be perfect. It's amazing how users or customers have a tendency to do things that we don't expect. So, it's important to check on performance and to continue to refine the experience.

But this is really where the idea of starting small and

evolving your voice app over time can be a game changer. By having a focused launch with defined metrics for success, you can see some clear results. And you can do that by looking at the data that comes from your skill or your experience, depending on what you have measured.

Look everything that is available about the voice app. Don't just look at how long users are spending on a skill or just the singular questions. But look at how those pieces show a whole experience. We start asking ourselves questions like:

Is this the usage behavior expected?

Was there a spot where users got hung up or lost?

Are there entry or exit utterances that were missed?

Are there new tasks that audiences are trying to do?

Are there return users? How frequently?

What are the paths they are taking?

Are they going to somewhere else and do we need to reconcile that?

Where are users exiting?

How are users closing off?

What is triggering bounced requests?

What is triggering error messages?

As you identify and implement simple improvements and enhancements, you will start to build trust with your user. By demonstrating an ability to fulfill the initial purpose you can start to get more complex. Because of that goodwill from the previous good experience, there will be some tolerance that your users will have if a new feature doesn't work quite right from the start. Over time, users will become accustomed to using that voice app and will continue to get comfortable using it.

When you apply the entire process from start to finish, and

you've built something based on your audience's needs and your business objectives, a couple of great things happen. First and foremost, you have happy customers. So internal stakeholders are pleased, especially when they're seeing results from it. Your audience is happy because you have created a positive customer experience overall. And ultimately that's what we're trying to do with Voice: create positive customer experiences and outcomes so that both the organization and the audience get value out of what we're creating.

SHAPING YOUR STRATEGY WITH THE VOICE EXPERIENCE FRAMEWORK

CHAPTER 22

3 QUESTIONS TO SHAPE YOUR VOICE STRATEGY

Having a process arms a team with an implementation plan and an understanding of how you will progress from concept/idea to launch to ongoing support. However, it's critical to have a strategy that holistically guides all the efforts in play. Similar to how a conductor orchestrates so that each instrument section works in concert with the other, your strategy helps keep your channels working in unison. While it's necessary to have a voice strategy, it cannot be forgotten that it is a part of a larger overarching strategy.

Your content should strive to answer three basic questions:

Is this the right type of business?

Can they help me solve my problem?

Why do I want to use them versus someone else?

But your voice strategy needs to answer a slightly different set of questions to be able to accomplish that:

Who is my audience and what are their problems and needs?

What are the business objectives of my organization that can be achieved by solving those problems? Which of those objectives am I trying to achieve using Voice?

How am I solving my customer's problems now? What of that can I use to inform a Voice driven experience or solution?

CHAPTER 23

KNOW YOUR AUDIENCE

Being customer first applies to all aspects of an organization so it shouldn't be any surprise that a voice strategy starts with your audience and their needs. You need to have a clear understanding of your audience and the problems you are trying to solve for them.

Who is your audience?

What are their needs and pain points?

What does a typical customer's journey look like?

What are they trying to do or what information do they need?

What content are they already viewing and engaging with frequently?

Your organization should have some or all of this information. If it doesn't, getting this information should be a priority because it's not just important for Voice, it's important for all marketing and customer experience efforts.

There are a few ways you can go about getting at this information to understand your audience. First and foremost, if you have the opportunity, talk to your audience directly. Direct research and interviews are the best way to get at what their challenges are, what their needs are, their frustrations, and how your solution may actually mitigate some of those challenges. Talking with them also uncovers the actual language and words they're using.

Knowing how your audience asks for things, calls products, and talks about their challenges informs what words and language your experience uses. By using their words, you will be able remove a layer of "translation" which will make your message that much clearer.

If you don't have any way to talk directly to your customer, then talk to your customer support folks. They can be a great resource because they are the people on the front lines every day talking to customers. They have first hand knowledge of what questions keep coming up, the frustrations expressed, the challenges had, and the language used. If you can't talk to the customer support folks, then see if you can get the call center transcripts.

Another group that's really great for customer insights is your sales force. They're out on the front lines as well, talking directly to customers. They have a really good handle on the challenges, how people are voicing their frustrations, how they actually view the competitors, and how they actually talk about their business problems. The sales force is often an untapped resource. But because product, marketing, sales, and customer support are typically siloed, no one's really talking to each other and exchanging information. Reaching across the silos is a great way to get at customer information if you can't do first hand research and build relationships across your own organization.

Another avenue you can take is social listening. It's much more observational because you really can't ask questions (although sometimes the opportunity presents itself) but you do get unbiased input. This is again helpful for understanding how your audiences talk about their problems and needs as well as knowing what they view as a priority. Sometimes you can find out that something you thought was a major gap is something that is acceptable to not have but there is another need that absolutely has to be fulfilled. This information is invaluable because later when you are developing a road map, you can prioritize features by your user's need versus novelty or vanity.

When you are doing this research, don't just strive to confirm assumptions but really try to build a robust profile of your audience. You want to go beyond demographics and superficial characteristics and dig into their core needs and wants. It's not as important to know the exact age of your audience as it is to know if their age plays into their preference for how they get notifications or how they seek out solutions. You want to get towards building a task and need driven profile because those will be the things you reference when you're building conversation flows later.

Once you have compiled all this research, make it available to your entire team. Don't lock it away in files or in someone's Sharepoint folder. Create audience personas (you may have more than one) and make them accessible to everyone. In fact, give them to everyone and make sure people know where they can locate the information behind them. Far too often this information gets captured and then locked away in one department so that teams start creating their own user personas. It's very difficult to be consistent if there are several different audience personas being used by different departments.

CHAPTER 24

UNDERSTAND YOUR BUSINESS OBJECTIVES & GOALS

As you come to understand your audience's needs and tasks, start thinking about the purpose your business serves and how it is solving the problems that your audience research identified.

Most every brand has goals built around growing its business. This can be done by increasing revenue or reducing costs. There's a host of ways to achieve both. Improving customer experience to win and retain customers is an obvious path to increasing revenue. Improving employee productivity can clearly reduce costs.

Although your strategy may be customer first, how you serve audience needs should not conflict with your business goals. Having clarity on what the business outcomes need to be helps ensure that. Those objectives can also inform how you measure the impact of your strategies and tactics.

Understanding those goals and the strategies that are in place to achieve them will also help identify areas where a voice strategy could be applied. For example, using Voice to create operational efficiencies to improve employee productivity might contribute to better customer service that results in increased customer retention.

CHAPTER 25

KNOW HOW YOU ARE SOLVING YOUR CUSTOMER'S PROBLEMS NOW

Chances are, your business is already solving a number of your customers' problems. Understanding how you are solving those problems now enables you to identify the opportunities where Voice can help reduce friction or increase efficiency.

Looking to existing processes and communications also helps you understand what is working or what might be impacted by the introduction of a Voice experience. While it's tempting to just look at external facing processes and materials you should also look internally. You might learn that what you thought was something to be solved by Voice actually is something that will require a change in protocol, additional training, and a Voice experience for customers.

The goal is to uncover what you can so that you have as much reference material as possible. This will help you start to prioritize parts of your strategy when it comes time to apply it. It also will provide reference information the team can draw upon when they are building actual Voice experiences which will help with efficiency and consistency.

CHAPTER 26

THE VOICE EXPERIENCE FRAMEWORK

Now that you know your audience, understand your business goals and objectives and understand how customer problems are currently being solved, you can use that to build out your Voice strategy. To make it easier we have developed a framework for planning and creating useful and usable Voice experiences by:

Identifying your audience's key tasks & information needs by customer journey phase

Understanding what content you have and what you need to create

Determining possible use cases for Voice

PRAGMATIC VOICE EXPERIENCE FRAMEWORK

VALUE PROPOSITION: What is your brand's unique selling proposition/value proposition to the consumer/user?

CORE STRATAEGY: What is the unifying brand strategy to convey that value proposition to achieve business goals?

CUSTOMER JOURNEY PHASE:

QUESTIONS	MESSAGES
What are the questions your users will ask during this phase?	What brand messages should the answers align with?

USER TASKS	CALLS TO ACTION
What tasks would a user want to do during this phase?	What behaviors do we want the user to take?

EXISTING CONTENT
What existing content can be used to answer the questions & help them complete their tasks?

CONTENT GAPS
What content is needed or missing to answer questions and help users complete their tasks?

WHERE VOICE FITS (USE CASES)
What ways could a voice application make a task easier? What problems can a voice application solve?

Fig 26.1 Illustration of the Voice Experience Framework.

We include the brand's value proposition and core strategy at the top of the worksheet as reminders of those important unifying pieces of the strategy. The value proposition is the brand's unique selling proposition (USP) to the consumer. The USP is what sets the brand apart in the marketplace and is something that the brand can solely "own." The core strategy is the unifying brand strategy being used to communicate that value proposition.

This framework uses the phases of the customer journey to make is easier to prioritize and focus on specific areas of the experience. A lot of times purchase and consideration come to the top. But there are times where depending on how your customer journey is put together, it's appropriate to look at where awareness or where retention comes into play.

When working with this framework, you can focus on a single phase of the customer journey or you can work across the entire journey. When it comes to the phases, you can start with the standard phases (Awareness,

Consideration, Purchase, Retention) or you can tailor them to your own specific journey map. It all depends if you need to address one specific phase where there is drop off or if you are trying to look holistically to understand where there are gaps in your experience.

Once we have set up the top portion of the framework by adding in our value proposition, core strategy, and determining what phase or phases of the customer journey will be included, we can move on to working through the sections under each phase.

Because we are focused on our user, we start with their tasks, needs and actions. First start with what Questions and Tasks the user will be asking during this phase. This helps us to start framing our content and solutions in terms of what the audience wants to know versus what we want to tell them about the brand. If the content is talking at the audience versus answering their questions and needs, then it really isn't an engaging conversation.

Your audience research will be able to help you get as specific as needed to be relevant and helpful:

Audience Goals (What are they trying to do?) will inform the Tasks for each phase.

Audience Needs (What do they need to be able to complete their tasks?) will inform Questions.

Audience Behavior Goals (What actions do we want them to take?) will inform the Calls to Action.

For example, under the Awareness phase, the Questions could be general inquiries that someone would ask if they were just learning about your brand or company:

Who is this brand?

What products or services do they sell?

What makes them different?

The Tasks could be:

Finding where the nearest location is to them

Visiting the company website to start to learn more about the company and its products or services (perhaps its story)

Reading relevant content the company has created or sponsored

The Calls to Action could then be:

Find a store, restaurant, office, etc. (depending on how/ where you conduct business)

Sign up for our newsletter

Read our latest blog

As you work through Calls to Action, keep yourself aligned with the Tasks. You'll quickly realize that Awareness tasks don't always line up with a drive to purchase. Thinking about the relationship of the phases as a progression can help re-frame your calls to action as how you move your audience from one phase to the next versus how you make a sale.

Once the customer information has been mapped out, then focus turns back to the brand.

Messages: What brand messages align with the answers to the audience's questions during that phase?

Content: What existing content can be used or leveraged and what new content do we need to create to fill in content gaps?

Going back to our Awareness example, some possible ways that the Message could align: "We have what you need for your X." and "We deliver expert service and advice like no other X." It's okay during this part to be brand-centric. Your final copy or experience might not be but at this stage, the goal is aligning your brand values or attributes to the task.

This shouldn't be a forced fit but a natural alignment. If it's a stretch at this stage, chances are that it will feel like a stretch or forced in the experience or worse, will come off as in-genuine so that it hurts your brand's credibility.

After completing the four quadrants, the result should be specific actions and tasks for each phase of the journey (side note: there will always be exceptions where a task happens in two phases but those should be exceptions, not the norm). Not only does this help with the focus of your journey phases but it also helps with identifying what content makes sense for each phase.

When we are starting to assess what existing content could work at each phase, the purpose is to find what can be leveraged for efficiency and consistency. This is content you can start with but know that it's just a starting point. It will require revising and editing to work in a voice experience or probably any other channel (you wouldn't copy and paste brochure copy on a web page, would you?). Some of this will come from a content audit or from what was discovered during the research around how the organization is already solving customer problems and information needs.

Keeping with the Awareness example, existing content could include:

Company brand video

Commercials (radio and television)

Digital advertising assets

Internal training materials for the sales force

Parts of a call center script

Press releases or analyst briefings

Blog posts and articles

Store list

Basically, all the content pieces you have created that help tell the story about who your company is and what makes it different from its competitors.

You may find you have a lot more than you expected. You might also find that one phase has an overwhelming amount of content while another phase has very little. Or you might find that in all of the content you have for one phase, you have been answering only some of the questions and facilitating a few of the tasks. These are your content gaps. Depending on priorities, you can make plans on how to fill the content gaps.

With the Questions, Tasks, Calls to Action, and content needs determined, we can start to identify where Voice can improve an experience or reduce friction (by the way, it won't make sense for everything). At this stage, we're simply finding the possible use cases for Voice.

Looking back at our Awareness example, we could solve for someone wanting to talk to an associate to learn more about the company by creating a simple Question and Answer experience that can live on Alexa and Google

Assistant. Maybe there's a relevant "how to" angle where there's a guided activity or relevant tips of the day to fuel a Flash Briefing. It could even be podcast content.

One additional piece you can add after you have your Voice use cases is a section for Technical Requirements or Considerations. This is where you would list the technical needs that are required to support any of the Voice use cases. It could be as simple as mapping out the need for experiences for the voice assistants to be supported or the systems that might have to pass information. This not only helps with building out the technical requirements needed, it will also potentially start the process of understanding what would align with the "crawl, walk, or run" evolution of an experience. Something might seem simple as a use case but then as the flow is talked out, you might find that three different back end systems have to talk to each other and that won't be nearly as simple as first thought. As you do that, you start to build your road map.

Once you have filled out this entire framework, you will

have a lot of information to form your strategy. You will have some relevant use cases for Voice. You also will have a clear view into where there are some content gaps and where perhaps you've actually got more than enough content. It's helpful to see that because it will put you in a position to gut check why you have so much content in one phase and a lot less in another. It might be that you keep creating content because you aren't getting conversions and need to refine your message. Or you might ask yourself if the team is creating content that's providing value and solving these questions or are they creating content out of habit, not need. Because you don't have to keep answering a question with new content if the existing answers get it right and the audience is understanding them. You also will be able to see if you're really heavying up on content to drive conversion in the purchase phase but maybe aren't doing enough during Consideration or Retention.

Regardless if you have focused on one phase of the customer journey or have decided to get full holistic view, you will have this lovely spreadsheet full of a lot of answers, information, and use cases. The natural, sane response will be that there is no possible way to do all the things that you have uncovered. This is when we do a prioritization exercise based on a content prioritization template developed by Meghan Casey in her book The Content Strategy Toolkit.

FEATURE/USE CASE PRIORITIZATION EXERCISE

GUIDE	FOCUS
Feature/use case important to your users and necessary for you to provide, but not beneficial to the business	Feature/use case most important to the business and our users
NOPE	DRIVE
Feature/use case that doesn't fulfill a user need or business goal	Feature/use case you may want to point users to once you've met their initial need

USER NEEDS

BUSINESS VALUE →

Fig 26.2 Visual: Prioritization Exercise based on Meghan Casey's Content Prioritization Template from The Content Toolkit)

This prioritizes your use cases on two axes: User Needs and Business Value and then divides that area into four quadrants that enable you to map out what is important and valuable to the user and business. This helps you ground your priorities on user and business need versus the tempting "wouldn't it be cool" category. So, we have four distinct groupings:

Guide: This is something that is higher in user need and although not high in business value is a necessity to the user. This could be something that explains terminology or provides your audience with information that helps them move from Awareness to Consideration. Or it can simply be instructional content.

Focus: High in user need and business value, this is what is important to the business and the user. This where you would place ways to purchase or convert but also anything that is going to benefit both users and business.

Drive: These are the things that have low user need but

higher business value. This could be features or content where you can point users to once you have met the initial need that brought them to you in the first place. It might be an up sell or additional ways to use your product. Something that wouldn't drive initial purchase but continues the relationship.

Nope: This is what has low business value and low user need. It doesn't help the user and it doesn't really help the business with any of its goals. This could be something that's required for compliance or legal reasons. It might be something mandated by corporate that satisfies an internal mandate. We call it "Nope" because we want to keep it to a minimum so that resources can be available for supporting the other three quadrants. (We have tried thinking of a gentler term but as we reflect upon our previous experiences during our careers, "Nope" is probably the best label.)

After you've gone through the worksheet and the prioritization exercise you should have the makings of a fairly robust road map with some prioritization. Both working together paint a picture of what aligns to the business goals, what aligns to customer needs and what's going to improve employee productivity or improve the customer experience.

FEATURE/USE CASE ROADMAP

CRAWL	WALK	RUN
Feature/use case most important to your users (and your business) Pick 3-4 things will have the biggest, most immediate impact.	Feature/use case optimizations from the crawl phase and any remaining items that you didn't include in the crawl phase.	Now that you have an established baseline, add feature/use case to enhance your audiences experience

Fig 26.3 Visual: Feature/Use Case Road map.

The resulting actions and tactics are tied back to the overarching strategy so that you're working with a voice strategy that can be brought to life. The tactics are also tied back to the objectives so there is a clear path forward that's measurable.

At the end of the day we want you to be able to tell a story that starts with what you know about your customers, what you know about your business, and then leads into how you are going to serve your customer and therefore serve your business for success.

How you present all that information depends entirely upon your leadership and your team. The worksheets and their components give you the information you need but, it could very well be that you need to condense it down into a very succinct PowerPoint presentation. Or you might need to then start crafting user stories so that your team can start to build out a delivery plan. It depends entirely upon your leadership team, how your team wants this information distilled, and how many artifacts you want to generate.

CONSIDERATIONS FOR CREATING VOICE EXPERIENCES

CHAPTER 27

PRAGMATIC CONSIDERATIONS FOR CREATING VOICE EXPERIENCES

Voice presents an opportunity to provide a new way for audiences to interact with a brand or service in a way that's incredibly exciting. When we start with initial brainstorms around possible use cases, our clients and partners' eyes often light up with enthusiasm. It's a fun exercise.

However, it is quite easy to be swept up in the ideas and forget some of the realities. There are a lot of considerations that come into play but there are a few that we especially want to call out as you start to navigate introducing Voice to your organization or quite honestly talk about even if you already are using Voice in your organization.

One of the questions we are often asked by someone who is developing their Voice experience is which platform should they use. Should they start with Alexa or Google Assistant? What about Bixby? Sometimes the question is if they should be considering those platforms at all. Our answer is always the same: It depends.

It depends if you are looking to a create something so you can start to lay a foundation of audio content for the Voice web, if you're wanting to create something new that won't be a huge effort to plan and implement, or if you're looking to integrate Voice into something that exists digitally or as an app on smartphones. Our recommendation is to start with where your audience is and how they are using what you already have. How and where your audience is going to be using this experience will also guide what devices and interfaces make the most sense.

There are some very compelling reasons to leverage the

voice assistants. There's an existing infrastructure and a lot of helpful templates to facilitate creation. They already have a following and a sizable installed base of users. Amazon and Google have a robust range of devices for your users as well. But then your experience will then be living within that ecosystem and a set of rules that's primarily out of your control.

But with the freedom of creating something outside of Amazon, Google, or Samsung's ecosystems, come other trade-offs.

Having your own separate Voice experience means that you're going to have to ask someone to either download something, update an app, or if you're thinking really big you could be actually even asking them to buy a whole new device. Those are some of the limitations that you should think through as you start to consider implementation outside the existing voice assistant platforms.

If you land on developing for the existing voice assistants, you can move over into implementation options. Not every experience requires custom development. Depending on your experience's purpose and features, it's possible to leverage one of the many voice experience platforms that are already in-market. Most of these work similarly to web content management systems and can be quite turnkey to use. Some even have features that can enable lead generation.

One other aspect of voice experience software platforms that can be helpful is that many work across Amazon Alexa, Google Assistant and soon Samsung Bixby as well. Currently because of market share in the U.S., companies are focusing on Amazon Alexa and Google Assistant. Regardless, it's important to focus on the voice assistant(s) your audience is using the most.

Then there's the topic of sonic branding. If you don't already have some sort of audio manifestation of your brand such as a spokesperson or something along those lines, you're going to be adding a brand-new dimension to your brand, so you are going to want to do a very thorough exploration. As sonic branding becomes more understood, its impact and value is also going to expand and grow. To do it properly, you will want to give as much attention to your sonic brand as you did your visual brand. In many cases the visual branding will no longer be there, so you have to work with someone who can help you navigate translating the visual into the sonic.

Now if you already have a speaking brand character (like Tony the Tiger or Flo from Progressive) or a spokesperson, some of that work has been done. But there are many other aspects to a sonic brand system that can go beyond the actual voice of the experience. Entry, exit, and confirmation tones can be included. Background music developed specifically for a brand can not only convey and reinforce aspects of a brand personality (warm, friendly, confident, etc.), it can also save money over time when used across channels, especially in media. Know that there is an art and science to sonic branding that an expert can help a brand navigate for best results.

Another aspect of sound that should be considered is the decision around where the "brand" voice will be used, where the device voice will come into play, and how your experience will handle the obvious difference between them. There's a few instances where this is merely a confirmation of where recorded audio will be included but if you're planning to have user provided information, you may need to think about how you handle the co-existence of the device voice with your brand voice. Having the device voice intermingling with the brand voice to confirm user provided information can be very jarring to the user or just hurt the overall perception of a smooth experience.

By the way, using the voice assistant or device voice doesn't mean that you are off the hook for sonic branding. This is where a sonic brand system can provide other audio cues that you can use to make your brand and your experience distinct even in a bit of a generic space even if it isn't a spokesperson. Again, that's when it's important to bring in an expert because they understand the nuances of sounds that we're only beginning to learn.

Beyond development platforms and branding, there are other additional questions you should be asking throughout the entire process. These are focused more around ethics and inclusivity. They should be asked early and often because they help guide us to not only solve problems but solve them well.

How does this truly solve my audiences' problems? We should make sure we are solving the spirit of the problem and not just the short-term fix.

Can everyone in my audience truly use this solution? Are there any "edge cases" I am missing? It's important to continually ask If the problem is being solved for every audience member and not just a portion of it. In the user experience community, there is a saying that edge cases define the border of how much of your audience you care about. Harsh as it sounds, there is a truth to it. When we think about solutions in terms of who can and who can't use it, there will always be an implied challenge to develop a more elegant solution (not an accommodation) to make the "can't" population smaller.

Is there any way this solution can be used in a harmful way? What could be unintended consequences that comes with using this solution? We have to challenge ourselves to break from the optimism of a solution and make sure that on the flip-side we are aware of the vulnerabilities or inadvertent trade offs that come with using our solution. We have to think about the risks as well as the rewards (sometimes more so about the risks).

While some of these questions can venture into more serious topics, it's important to have those conversations now while you're in the design and the planning stage versus having to figure out a work around after something has launched. It's amazing and fun to think through all of the ways that we're going to be able to change the world and make it a better place but, it's also important to think about the flip side so that as we do that we really do help move

towards a more inclusive and helpful world.

CHAPTER 28

FINAL THOUGHTS

Scot and I hope you found this book useful and you'll use it to create audience pleasing Voice experiences. We covered a lot of concepts in this book and you might be feeling a little overwhelmed right now. Not to worry, we're here to help.

If you have questions, feel free to contact us:

Email: **susan@pragmatic.digital** Twitter: **@SJW75**

Email: **scot@pragmatic.digital** Twitter: **@scotwestwater**

Website: www.pragmatic.digital

Company Twitter: @PragmaticDigitl

If you want more in-depth learning about the concepts in this book, Voice Masters offers an online course for individuals and teams who want further guidance as they develop their own Voice strategies. We also offer bootcamps and in-person workshops. **You can learn more at www.Voicemasters.ai**

For help with creating your own strategy, we are available to consult on projects to get you on your way with Voice even faster. **To learn more about working with us, feel free to send us a note and we'll be in touch.**

Thank you so much for reading.

Cheers!

Susan & Scot Westwater

#voicefirst

WORKS CITED

1 Desjardins, Jeff. "The Rising Speed of Technological Adoption." Visual Capitalist, 14 Feb. 2018, https://www.visualcapitalist.com/rising-speed-technological-adoption/.

2 "US Smart Speaker Users, by Activity, 2019 (% of Smart Speaker Users)." EMarketer, https://www.emarketer.com/chart/228974/us-smart-speaker-users-by-activity-2019-of-smart-speaker-users. Accessed 13 Nov. 2019.

3 "New Data on Voice Assistant SEO Is a Wake-up Call for Brands." Voicebot.Ai, 9 July 2019, https://voicebot.ai/2019/07/09/new-data-on-voice-assistant-seo-is-a-wake-up-call-for-brands/. Accessed 13 Nov. 2019.

4 "Voice Technology Investment Within the Next 1 to 2 Years According to US Senior Decision-Makers, Aug 2018 (% of Respondents)." EMarketer, https://www.emarketer.com/chart/223800/voice-technology-investment-within-next-1-2-years-according-us-senior-decision-makers-aug-2018-of-respondents. Accessed 13 Nov. 2019.

5 Tripathy, Abinash. "The Contact Center Is Having Its Model T Moment." Forbes, https://www.forbes.com/sites/forbestechcouncil/2017/12/07/the-contact-center-is-having-its-model-t-moment/. Accessed 13 Nov. 2019.

WORKS CONSULTED

Atherton, Mike, and Carrie Hane. Designing Connected Content: Plan and Model Digital Products for Today and Tomorrow. New Riders, 2018.

Canalys Newsroom- Canalys: Global Smart Speaker Installed Base to Top 200 Million by End of 2019. https://www.canalys.com/newsroom/canalys-global-smart-speaker-installed-base-to-top-200-million-by-end-of-2019. Accessed 13 Nov. 2019.

Casey, Meghan. The Content Strategy Toolkit: Methods, Guidelines, and Templates for Getting Content Right. New Riders, 2015.

Covert, Abby, and Nicole Fenton. How to Make Sense of Any Mess. 2014.

Edison Research. The Smart Audio Report. Spring 2019, 7 Nov. 2019, p. 36, https://www.nationalpublicmedia.com/wp-content/uploads/2019/06/The_Smart_Audio_Report_Spring_2019.pdf.

Hall, Erika. Conversational Design. A Book Apart. 2018.

Halvorson, Kristina, and Melissa Rach. Content Strategy for the Web. 2nd ed, New Riders, 2012.

Klein, Laura. Build Better Products: A Modern Approach to Building Successful User-Centered Products. Rosenfeld Media, 2016.

Knapp, Jake, et al. Sprint: How to Solve Big Problems and Test New Ideas in Just Five Days. First Simon & Schuster hardcover edition, Simon & Schuster, 2016.

Krug, Steve. Don't Make Me Think, Revisited: A Common Sense Approach to Web Usability. Third edition, New Riders, 2014.

McGovern, Gerry. TOP TASKS: A How-to Guide. SILVER BEACH, 2018.

McGovern, Gerry. Transform: A Rebel's Guide for Digital Transformation. 2016.

Minsky, Laurence, and Colleen Fahey. Audio Branding: Using Sound to Build Your Brand. 1st Edition, Kogan Page Ltd, 2017.

"Nearly Half of American Households Will Own a Smart Speaker by 2019." Fortune, https://fortune.com/2018/09/10/smart-speaker-ownership-amazon-echo-apple-homepod/. Accessed 13 Nov. 2019.[A1]

Pearl, Cathy. Designing Voice User Interfaces: Principles of Conversational Experiences. First edition, O'Reilly, 2017.

"The 2019 Voice Report – Bing and Microsoft." Microsoft Advertising, https://about.ads.microsoft.com/en-us/insights/2019-voice-report. Accessed 13 Nov. 2019.

ABOUT THE AUTHORS

Susan and Scot Westwater are the co-founders of Pragmatic Digital, a consultancy who helps clients identify and solve their marketing and customer experience problems by leveraging the Voice channel.

As part of its approach, Pragmatic Digital has developed a proven process that enables our clients to create, review and deploy Voice experiences that are on-brand while delivering against audience needs. Their primary goal for clients is to create Voice experiences that align with business objectives while delivering value by being useful and usable to their audiences.

Susan has been working in the fields of digital strategy and content strategy for the past 20+ years. Her experience with digital strategy dates back to when websites were the "hot" new thing so her knowledge is based upon actual practice and implementation. Working with designers and writers, she has developed content strategies that have established brands and customer experiences for organizations across a variety of industries. With a career that includes agency and client-side experience, Susan has managed global, national and regional brand launches and content initiatives. She is also a leadership member of Women in Voice.

Scot draws upon his 20+ years of design, user experience and digital strategy to help clients create relevant and useful applications of existing and emerging technologies to enhance their overall customer experiences. Like Susan, Scot helped clients navigate the advent of the web, mobile, and now, Voice.He is a passionate marketer dedicated to helping companies better understand their customers' challenges and needs.

Susan and Scot have authored a number of articles and ebooks focused on the intersection of business strategy and Voice technology. They have also presented their talks and workshops at a number of events including Voice Summit and were a part of the SEM Rush's first ever Global Marketing Day.

Voice Strategy: Creating Useful and Usable Voice Experiences is their first book together.